Crime Scene Whodunits

Dr. Quicksolve Mini-Mysteries

Jim Sukach

Illustrated by Tatjana Mai-Wyss

Sterling Publishing Co., Inc.
New York

Library of Congress Cataloging-in-Publication Data

Sukach, Jim.
  Crime scene whodunits : Dr. Quicksolve mini-mysteries / Jim
Sukach ; illustrated by Tatjana Mai-Wyss.
      p. cm.
  Includes index.
  ISBN 1-4027-0365-1
1. Puzzles. 2. Detective and mystery stories. I. Title: Dr.
Quicksolve mini-mysteries. II. Title.
GV1507.D4 S825 2002
793.73—dc21

                                                    2002151752

10 9 8 7 6 5 4 3 2 1

Published by Sterling Publishing Co., Inc.
387 Park Avenue South, New York, NY 10016
© 2003 by James Richard Sukach
Distributed in Canada by Sterling Publishing
% Canadian Manda Group, One Atlantic Avenue, Suite 105
Toronto, Ontario, Canada M6K 3E7
Distributed in Great Britain and Europe by Chris Lloyd
at Orca Book Services, Stanley House, Fleets Lane, Poole
BH15 3AJ, England
Distributed in Australia by Capricorn Link (Australia) Pty. Ltd.
P.O. Box 704, Windsor, NSW 2756, Australia

Printed in China
All rights reserved

Sterling ISBN 1-4027-0365-1

Contents

Introduction

Join famous detective Dr. Jeffrey Lynn Quicksolve and his friends as they search the evidence for clues to fight crime. Follow the most brilliant, most unusual, and funniest detective, Elliott Savant, as he appears to stumble his way through to solve a crime.

Detective Elliott Savant, who looks more like a mad scientist than a detective with his long, curly black hair and his bushy, black mustache, is a man of unusual intelligence and devotion to duty. But his penchant for deep thinking leads him to forget certain things others might consider significant, such as where he is and what he is doing at the moment. And so the brilliant detective has been assigned an assistant, a rather nervous Officer Boysenberry, to look after him.

Elliott may arrive on his motorcycle wearing an unusual helmet with colorful plumes, or on Mollie, his dancing mule, or driving one of his antique cars, and he may drive Officer Boysenberry playfully to his wits' end. But the one thing that is certain is that Detective Elliott Savant will solve the most unusual cases in a most unusual and hilarious manner.

Join him, and you can solve these mysteries too!

Vanished Vase

It was still early in the morning, and Mrs. Penelope Smithsony was waiting at the door of her huge white-pillared mansion as Dr. J. L. Quicksolve walked up the steps. "I've been robbed!" she told him. "Burglars!"

They went into a parlor where hot tea was waiting for them. "Tell me about it," Dr. Quicksolve said, sipping his tea. "What did they take?"

"That's the funny part," Penelope said, though she did not really think it was funny. "I guess they knew just what to take. At least I think they did. The only thing missing is my antique vase. I was thinking of selling it. I just called an antique dealer last week for an estimate. I know nothing at all about antiques. I was

6

going to take it to him this afternoon."

"Who might have known about this vase and that it might be sold soon?" the detective asked.

"Well, just family, a few friends, and, of course, the maid, the butler, and the cook," Penelope said.

"Were any of these people here yesterday?" Dr. Quicksolve asked.

"I was home alone all day except for the help. They were all here part of the day, but they are not here now," Penelope said.

"Let's talk to them when they arrive today," Dr. Quicksolve said.

Hilary, the maid, was the first to arrive. She acted very surprised to hear about the stolen vase. "I was glad it was going to be sold," she told Dr. Quicksolve. "One less thing to dust. But I don't know who would steal it. It was only worth about twenty dollars," she said. "It was not worth stealing."

The butler said, "I was always nervous when I was around that vase. It had to be worth a lot of money. It was obviously old and very beautiful."

The cook was also surprised to hear there had been a burglary. His statement was, "I am surprised they just took the vase. I guess I would have taken the silverware and a few other things. There are several valuable paintings in the house." That earned him a dirty look from his employer.

"I think you would have taken a lot more too," Dr. Quicksolve said. "But I think I need to take Hilary down to the station for more questioning."

"I can't believe Hilary would take something from the mansion that doesn't belong to her," Penelope said.

Why did Dr. Quicksolve suspect the maid?

Answer on page 90.

Chewing Gum Art

"**I knew he would be a famous artist** some day, and here he is with his own show," Benjamin Clayborn Blowhard said as he walked into the Mason Jarse Museum with Sergeant Rebekah Shurshot, Dr. J. L. Quicksolve, and Junior. They walked into the huge main gallery where Blowhard's "discovery," an artist known as Thunk, displayed his chewing gum art.

"I'll never forget discovering him in Paris," Blowhard said. Looking like Teddy Roosevelt giving a speech with his western hat pinned up on one side, he continued. "I had just stepped on a piece of gum as I backed up to look at the Eiffel Tower. My shoe was stuck to the pavement. It actually came off my foot. It took two hands and a big tug to get my shoe off the pavement because of the huge, blue wad of chewing gum I had stepped on. Suddenly I heard a voice behind me, 'Monsieur! How wonderful! May I have it?' He told me how American tourists supplied him with the most wonderful bits of chewing gum that he collected to create his art."

They looked around the room in amazement as Blowhard continued talking. The walls were covered with pictures made of various colors of chewing gum. In the center were a dozen sculptures made completely out of thick masses of chewing gum. There were horses and dogs and figures of people greeting each other, dancing, and apparently singing to the sky with hands upraised and mouths wide open. Everything was made with chewing gum.

There were only two paintings in the room that were not part of the Thunk exhibit and not made of colorful wads of chewing gum. They were two large oil paintings by the famous Canadian artist Henry Felix. They were quite valuable, and Dr. Quicksolve noticed they were each tightly screwed to the wall with six screws along the edge of the picture frames. Although the prices on Thunk's chewing gum art were quite high, Dr. Quicksolve noticed they were not screwed to the wall. His friend Fred Fraudstop, an insurance investigator, had once told him that the screws told you which pieces of art the Mason Jarse Museum considered the most valuable.

Suddenly the lights went out. Ladies screamed. Everyone heard a strange whirring sound: Chrrrk! Chrrrk! Chrrrk! Then silence. The lights came back on. Everyone scanned the room quickly. The Thunk exhibition was apparently unmolested. Then Junior

said, "Look!" He pointed to the end of the large room. One of the Henry Felix paintings was missing.

Everyone was ordered to stay in the museum, and an investigation was begun. Museum employees and others said no one had left during or after the blackout.

"The paintings and the thieves must still be in the museum," Junior said.

Sergeant Shurshot said, "We have found two workmen in the building who say they were in separate rooms when the lights went out. Both of them had a drill that could have caused the whirring sounds we heard."

"The thief must have used a drill as an electric screwdriver to take the painting down," Junior said.

"One of those men must be the thief!" Blowhard announced, as if he had suddenly solved the crime all by himself.

"Not exactly," Dr. Quicksolve said.

What did Dr. Quicksolve mean?

Answer on page 90.

Cousin in Custody

Dr. J. L. Quicksolve was talking to a friend of his on the police force, Sergeant Lou Trusten, about a rash of murders in the area. The victims had all been high school and college girls. Apparently, they all had been picked up or kidnapped. They were taken somewhere and killed with a knife. Their bodies were then dumped out on a secluded road away from town.

Dr. Quicksolve enjoyed solving crimes…piecing the puzzle together. Though always serious business, it was also a kind of game for him. The bloody details of real murder were not fun…not a game to enjoy. They made the "game" serious, and winning the game before another murder became very important in situations like this one.

Another intriguing unpleasantness about this case was the fact that Sergeant Trusten's cousin was the suspect.

"I can't believe they picked up my cousin on suspicion of murder," Sergeant Trusten told Dr. Quicksolve.

Sergeant Trusten's cousin fit the description of someone seen with the last victim. His black convertible fit the description given by a friend of a previous victim who saw the young woman before she disappeared.

"He's just a typical teenager," Sergeant Trusten said. "He likes girls and hot rods. He's a little strange, but isn't

that normal for a nineteen-year-old boy?" he asked.

"Well, you can't always tell," Dr. Quicksolve said. "There is one thing about this kind of a case, with kidnappings and everything....There are too many ways to make a mistake. We should catch the bad guy. If your cousin is innocent, it shouldn't be too hard to prove it. Does he have an alibi?"

"No. That is a problem," the sergeant admitted. "We've been out of town, and he's been taking care of our house. He took really good care of it. He even painted the concrete floor in the basement after he cleaned it up. It looks great. He's very conscientious."

"Did you ask him to clean the basement?" Dr. Quicksolve asked.

"No. We just told him to clean up any messes he might make. He's a good kid," Sergeant Trusten said.

"I would like to see your house, Sergeant," Dr. Quicksolve said, "and I think you had better brace yourself."

What did Dr. Quicksolve suspect?

Answer on page 90.

Crime Time

Junior was in his garage pouring a thick white substance into a circular piece of cardboard when his friends, Skeeter and Prissy Powers, walked in. Junior looked up and said, "Hi, Skeeter. Hi Prissy. I think I found a footprint of a fox in my backyard."

"A fox?" Prissy said.

"Yes," Junior said, pushing the mold aside so he could give his attention to his friends.

"I have a problem," Skeeter said, "…a big problem."

"What is it?" Junior asked.

"You know that watch my Dad gave me for my birthday three years ago?" Skeeter said. He didn't wait for an answer. "John Bigdood stole it."

"How did he do that?" Junior asked.

"I guess it's my fault," said Prissy Powers, the prettiest girl on the cheerleading squad at school.

"How is it your fault?" Junior asked her.

"I borrowed Skeeter's watch to time our relay team. We're getting ready for the District Track Meet," she said.

"So John took it from you?" Junior asked.

"Well," Prissy began, "we were timing each other, and John was standing around making wisecracks."

"What did he say?" Junior asked.

"He said a lot of stuff. One of the girls pushed one of the buttons and the watch lit up. John said, 'I've got a watch just like that. I turn off the light at home and make monster noises to scare my little sisters. I time them to see how long it takes them to scream! It doesn't take long!' That guy makes me scream without turning

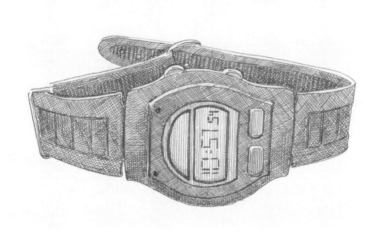

17

out the lights! I would like to turn out *his* lights!"

Junior was surprised to see Prissy so angry. It wasn't like her to get so upset. "But how did he get the watch?" Junior asked.

"Well," Prissy said, "We didn't actually see him take it. We finished practice, and we were doing our stretching when Skeeter came back to get his watch. John was gone, and so was the watch. He must have taken it!"

"We found him later," Skeeter said. "He was actually wearing the watch and showing it off to his friends! I told him that was my watch. He said it was his and I couldn't prove it was mine."

"Can't you do something, Junior?" Prissy said. "What about fingerprints? You can test for fingerprints!"

"It is too late for that," Skeeter said. "So many girls handled it...and John, too. He has probably even thought of that and wiped it clean, anyway."

"But he doesn't know how old it is. There may be something yet," Junior said.

What is Junior talking about?

Answer on page 90.

ℛobbins

ℬr. J. L. Quicksolve rang the doorbell of what looked like a typically modest ranch-style home in a neighborhood of large two-story colonials. Sergeant Rebekah Shurshot came to the door and escorted the famous detective into the house. They walked back deeper and deeper through room after room. Dr. Quicksolve could see that it must be one of the largest houses in the neighborhood, despite its appearance from the street. "Looks can be deceiving," the famous detective thought to himself. But he already knew that, and with three suspects to this burglary, he knew attempts at deception were sure to unfold.

"The robbery happened yesterday while the Robbinses were at an archery tournament in

Sherwood," Sergeant Shurshot explained as they proceeded through the living room. Dr. Quicksolve noticed several beautiful and original paintings. He also noted magnificent Persian rugs and a wonderful grand piano fitting quite nicely in its own large space in an open room with hardwood floors and large windows that lined the walls, exploding light across the floor and piano, making the room look wonderfully grand altogether.

"What was taken?" Dr. Quicksolve asked.

"Only money and jewelry," Sergeant Shurshot said. Sensing Dr. Quicksolve's curiosity about the large, valuable items that were left behind, she added, "A lot of money and jewelry."

They entered the dining room, where Officer Longarm sat talking to Mr. and Mrs. Robbins and their maid, Marian.

Dr. Quicksolve sat down immediately and turned to Mr. Robbins. "Tell me about the three suspects," Dr. Quicksolve said.

Mr. Robbins was thrown off balance and reacted nervously to the abrupt question.

"Well…I…there were three people who had access to the house," Mr. Robbins said. "They're the three suspects, but I doubt…"

"Tell me about them," Dr. Quicksolve said, "and why they had access to your home."

"Well," Mr. Robbins began, "our maid, Marian, was the only person who had a key, as far as we know. She wasn't really working, but she came to the house twice to let others in—a neighbor boy, John Little, whom we hired to water the plants and walk the turtle."

"And the other one," Officer Longarm said, "was

Alex Bell, who works for the phone company."

"We needed phone connections put in," Mrs. Robbins said. "A friend of ours has a nephew who works for the phone company while going to college. That's Alex. We arranged for Marian to let him in, too," she said.

"Apparently, Marian let John into the house at eight o'clock this morning. She waited for him to water the plants and walk the turtle. They both left at nine-fifteen," Officer Longarm said, reading from his notepad.

"Were they together for that period of time?" Dr. Quicksolve asked.

"No. The house is so big, and Marian said she had a few things to do. The money and jewelry were in an unlocked bureau drawer in the walk-in closet of the master bedroom."

"Either Marian or John could have gone in there?" Sergeant Shurshot asked.

"Yes," Officer Longarm replied.

"Why doesn't your maid do those chores?"

Detective Quicksolve asked Mrs. Robbins.

"She's deathly afraid of the turtle," Mrs. Robbins said, "and she can't reach all the plants. She likes letting repairmen in. I think she likes a man with a tool belt, the way some women like a man in uniform."

"And Mr. Bell?" Dr. Quicksolve said.

"That is where we see the real burglar," Mr. Robbins said. "I don't see why the sergeant suspects John or Marian. The repairman said he was actually confronted by the burglar, who must have wandered in through an open door."

"Mr. Bell said a tall masked man with a gun surprised him and locked him in the closet of the master bedroom. He claims this intruder took the money, locked him in the closet, and left," Officer Longarm said.

"Where was Marian while all this was going on?" Dr. Quicksolve asked.

"She had opened the door for the repairman and then left for about three hours or so. When she got back, she heard pounding and found the repairman in the closet. He'd been there for about two and a half hours," Officer Longarm said.

"So there are really four to suspect," Dr. Quicksolve said. "But, of course, it's the one whose name has such a familiar ring to it that arouses the greatest suspicion."

Who was Dr. Quicksolve talking about?

Answer on pages 90–91.

Deputy Dowd

Dr. J. L. Quicksolve and his son Junior buzzed along the highway. Junior loved tooling along the California coastline on the back of his dad's motorcycle. It was turning out to be a father-son trip to remember.

They had microphones attached to their motorcycle helmets so they could talk to each other and be heard over the sound of the wind blasting against them.

"We're going to stop at Bob Bullion's Safe-N-Sure Security Company," Dr. Quicksolve said. "He's a friend of mine. I think you'll be interested in seeing his company."

They slowed and turned off the highway and drove down a long drive and past a tall sign that said "Safe-

N-Sure."

They met Bob Bullion, who was excited about seeing an old friend and immediately offered to show them around.

"Your dad was out here before," Bob Bullion said to Junior as they walked down the hallway. "He kept me from hiring a dangerous criminal. The guy wanted to be a security guard on one of my armored trucks. Your dad picked up a clue that saved me from some possibly serious trouble. By the way, he e-mailed that you earned your Eagle rank in your Boy Scout Troop back there in Ann Arbor. That's quite an accomplishment!"

They stopped at a door marked "Private," and Bob took out a set of keys and unlocked the door. "Come in here," Bob said. "We're interviewing a man from Michigan right now. His name is Dowd. We can hear them, but they can't see or hear us."

It was a dark little room that had a row of chairs facing a long window. It had a one-way mirror that allowed them to see into the next room without being seen by the people in the other room. They could see two men through the glass in the next room. They were sitting at a table, talking to each other. One of them leaned back in his chair, taking notes on a clipboard he held on his lap with his right hand as he wrote with his left. Clipped to his lapel was a Safe-N-Sure identification tag with his picture on it. The other man was broad shouldered. His hair was cut very short, and he had a neat, thin mustache. He sat up straight in his chair and tapped his fingers lightly on the table as he answered the interviewer's questions.

"You wrote on your application that you were training to be a deputy for the Michigan State Police," the interviewer said.

"Yes," the man replied. "I was accepted for the job and started the training, but then we moved down here to California."

"So you did go through security clearance in Michigan, right?" the interviewer asked.

"Oh, yes. There was no problem with that. I worked for a private security company before that," Dowd said.

"It sounds good that he's already cleared," Bob Bullion said to Dr. Quicksolve and Junior.

"I don't think so," Junior said.

Why did Junior have doubts about Dowd?

Go with the Flow

The hard rain stopped as suddenly as it started two hours earlier, and the sun came out. Dr. J. L. Quicksolve was telling his son Junior how proud he was that Junior had earned the rank of Eagle Scout. Their friends, Sergeant Rebekah Shurshot and Detective Elliott Savant, sat in the back seat of Dr. Quicksolve's yellow VW Beetle as they drove home from the Boy Scout camp where Junior had received his award.

Sergeant Shurshot's cell phone buzzed. She answered it and then explained that there had been a robbery at a nearby gas station. A man had been wounded with a gunshot. Two men were seen running from the station. They had jumped into a pickup truck

27

with a camper unit on the back. What looked to be the truck was found at the edge of a state park.

They drove to the park and found Officer Longarm and a park ranger who told them they had three pairs of suspects. As they walked through the park, Sergeant Shurshot was careful to walk around the puddles left from the rain. Elliott walked right through them. Since he so often wore his trench coat and black galoshes, he did not worry about the wet weather. His mind did not seem to be on the weather conditions.

"We haven't seen anybody else," George Henry, the first suspect they questioned, told them. "My friend and I hiked in here last night. In spite of the rain, we've been fishing all day, and we were just about to eat a couple of them." They had a fire going and two fish were sizzling in a frying pan set over the campfire.

Two other men who were camping nearby were questioned inside their tent, where they sat on their cots with their boots nervously splashing in the wet grass. Todd Benz reached down to pick up his back-pack and put it up on the cot where it was dry. "We set up the tent this morning," he said. "Then we went for a hike. When the rain got real heavy, we found a wooden bridge over the stream. We stayed under that to wait out the downpour. When it eased up, we came back. We haven't been here long."

The last two campers were in a motor home. "We've been in here playing cards all day because of the rain," Jason Dealer said. "We haven't seen anything."

As the entourage of law officers walked past the second tent on their way back to the parking lot, Sergeant Shurshot said, "Well, all their splish-splashing makes these guys our number one suspects.

Should I take them in?"

"Some people say, 'Go with the flow,'" Detective Elliott Savant said. "Let's check that out." He walked around the tent looking down at the ground.

What evidence was Sergeant Shurshot talking about with her "splish-splash" comment? And what "flow" was Detective Elliott Savant talking about?

Answer on page 91.

When Turning Left Is Right

"There were bank robberies in Hartford, Kalamazoo, Battle Creek, and Jackson," Sergeant Shurshot said to Dr. J. L. Quicksolve, who was driving his bright yellow VW Beetle. "Each robbery hit a major city at exactly weekly intervals. Each city has been the next one directly east of the last one. The criminal is always alone and wearing a black baseball cap. He is so consistent, it almost looks like he either wants to be caught or he's taunting the police, thinking he's too smart for them."

Dr. Quicksolve stopped his car at a red light. He looked ahead where his street continued one-way for several blocks. He looked to his right and turned left onto the one-way street and headed west before the light changed.

"I still have trouble remembering when you can turn left on a red light after you stop," Sergeant Shurshot said.

"Well," Dr. Quicksolve said, "since we were turning from a one-way street onto a one-way street, it didn't matter. But the rule applies only to the street you're turning onto. It didn't really matter what kind of street we were turning from."

Sergeant Shurshot scratched her head. "It isn't like that in every state, though, is it?" she said.

"No. It's not always that way," Dr. Quicksolve said. He drove a block and turned right.

"We're driving the Beetle today because of those robberies," Dr. Quicksolve said. "Captain Blade asked me to drive you around and keep a lookout. He has every patrol car on the road today."

They noticed a tall man walking along the sidewalk with both of his hands stuck into the pockets of his dark coat. He wore a black baseball cap, and he was walking in the direction of the downtown bank.

"This looks suspicious," Sergeant Shurshot said.

Just as he reached the corner, Dr. Quicksolve pulled his car to the curb next to the man. He was tall enough that Dr. Quicksolve could look up at him and talk to him through the open moonroof.

"Say!" Dr. Quicksolve called to the man.

The man looked irritated. He hesitated. Then he stepped closer to the car and said, "What do you want?"

"Could you tell me how to get to the freeway? I'm turned around a bit," Dr. Quicksolve said.

"Sure," the man said. He pointed north, the

direction the car was facing. "Turn right here. Then turn right at the next corner."

"Thanks a lot," Dr. Quicksolve said. He turned right and stopped the car. "Call for backup," he said to Sergeant Shurshot.

Why was Dr. Quicksolve suddenly convinced this was a suspicious character?

Answer on page 91.

Friday Fudgesicle

Dr. J. L. Quicksolve pulled his yellow Beetle into the gas station/convenience store and was surprised to see two black-and-white police cars pull in right behind him with their blue lights flashing. He walked in and bought himself a cup of coffee, knowing he would forget why he stopped at the store once he started talking to his friends, Sergeant Rebekah Shurshot and Officer Longarm, who were climbing out of the two police cars.

Dr. Quicksolve greeted his friends and then listened quietly as they talked to Sidney Slug, who was explaining how his car had just been stolen.

"I work at the bank across the street," Sidney said. "I live about forty miles away, but I buy my gas here

every Friday after I get paid because it's cheaper here."

"So what happened?" Sergeant Shurshot asked.

"Well, I got out of my car to go in and get a fudgesicle. I always get a fudgesicle on Friday. I eat it while I'm pumpin' gas. I even do that in the winter," Sidney said. "Well, I started to walk back to my car when it started to pull away! Somebody was stealing it!"

Officer Longarm looked at Sergeant Shurshot and then at Sidney. "Did you get a look at the person who stole your car?" he asked Sidney.

"Yes. I did. I watched him race through that inter-section and get right on the highway heading south. I don't know where he was going, though. I don't know why he was heading south," Sidney said.

"But can you tell us what he looked like?" Officer Longarm persisted.

"Well, yes," Sidney said.

"What did he look like?" Longarm said.

"Kind of like you," Sidney said.

"Tall? Brown hair?" Officer Longarm said.

"Yes. Brown hair. He looked tall sittin' in the car. Yes," Sidney said slowly.

"What kind of car was it?" Sergeant Shurshot asked.

"Kind of like that one," Sidney said, indicating Dr. Quicksolve's VW. "Just like that one, really. Of course, mine's gone."

"I'll radio ahead," Sergeant Shurshot said, moving toward her patrol car. "The next exit from the freeway is twenty miles away. We may be able to get someone on the highway to cut him off."

Dr. Quicksolve got into Sergeant Shurshot's car on the passenger side. Sergeant Shurshot climbed in behind the wheel and started the engine.

"We might not have to be in too big of a hurry," Dr. Quicksolve said.

Why not be in a hurry?

Answer on pages 91–92.

Stalker

Prissy Powers, the cutest girl on the high school cheerleading squad and a good friend of Junior Quicksolve, was very upset when she ran up to Junior, who was standing in the hallway at his school locker.

"What's wrong?" Junior asked his friend.

"It's Aunt Lucy," she said. "Someone's been following her."

"But she's had stalkers following her before. That happens to a lot of movie stars like your aunt. That's why she has a bodyguard," Junior said.

"Yes, but this one has her worried. Her bodyguard and the police haven't been able to catch him. He is really making her nervous," Prissy said. "She saw him late last night. He seems to know when the bodyguard is around and when he's gone. This time he came up to the house and looked into the windows!"

"That is getting pretty serious. How does she know it's the same guy?" Junior asked.

"That's the thing," Prissy continued. "I think I know who it is!"

"How could you know that?" Junior asked, closing his locker and waiting for her answer.

"She knows it's the same guy because of the unusual car lights," Prissy said. "She heard him at the window and turned on the room lights. She just saw his back as he ran into the darkness. She heard a car door slam, and a few seconds later she saw the taillights of a car come on a little way up the street. It was already moving, so he must have started driving before he turned his lights on."

"So what did you decide from all that?" Junior asked.

"It was the lights," Prissy answered. "She saw the lights before. They were big, round, red lights with smaller round lights above those. You know who has a car like that!"

"John Bigdood," Junior said. "He doesn't come to school much, but he is a senior here. I think he works during school hours sometimes to help pay for that customized '59 Ford with the hot-rod engine. Maybe we should check out his locker."

"I know where it is," Prissy said. "It's by the girls' locker room. He likes to stand there and watch the girls walk by in their gym uniforms."

They found John Bigdood's locker easily enough. It had the initials "J. B." formed with chewing gum on the door. It also had a decal of a skull and crossbones.

"How are we going to get it open?" Prissy asked.

"No problem," Junior said. Just three steps ahead of her, he reached the locker, pulled a tool out of his pocket, and opened the door immediately.

"Let's see what's in here," Junior said, peering into the open locker. "A math book."

Prissy said, "That's a surprise."

Junior reached his hand into the locker and wiped a finger across the book. He showed his finger to Prissy. It was covered with dust. They both laughed. Then Junior brought out three other things and showed them to Prissy. There were a rolled-up movie magazine with a picture of Lucy Looker on the cover, a long, black-handled switchblade knife, and a small lightbulb.

"This looks like serious evidence," Junior said.

"That shows he had Aunt Lucy on his mind," Prissy said.

"That is not what I meant," Junior said. "I imagine a lot of high school guys have a picture of Lucy Looker."

"Then you mean the…"

"Yes," Junior said, "the lightbulb!"

What is Junior talking about?

Answer on page 92.

Convenience Store Panic

Officer Lurkin had been posted outside the Stop-Shop Convenience Store and Gas Station after it had been robbed three times. He wore gray coveralls and stood beneath the sign that displayed the current price of gasoline. He used a long pole to change the numbers. He hoped he wouldn't be identified as a police officer as he stood there all morning, munching donuts and changing the numbers around without ever changing the price of gasoline. Now he was talking to Officer Longarm, Dr. J. L. Quicksolve, and Sergeant Rebekah Shurshot in front of the store.

He said two men came running out of the store screaming. One man ran down a side street, and the other man jumped on a bicycle and headed south on

the main road. Officer Lurkin said he ran into the store
and found the clerk unconscious and lying on the
floor. The clerk was still lying in the store and unconscious, but medics who were attending to him said he
would be okay.

The two men had been rounded up and questioned.
"They each claim the other one pulled a knife on the
clerk and demanded money. The clerk fainted, and
both the criminal and the bystander panicked and ran
out the door screaming," Officer Lurkin explained.

"Did you find the money or the knife on either of
the men when they were caught?" Sergeant Shurshot
asked.

"No money was actually taken because of the panic,

and no knife has been found," Lurkin said.

"What did they have?" Dr. Quicksolve asked.

Officer Lurkin looked at his notepad. He said, "Well, the running man had his wallet, a comb, spare change, a little flashlight, a candy bar, and two watches. He said he forgot to pay for the candy bar."

"Two watches?" Sergeant Shurshot said.

"He said he's a salesman staying at a motel down the street. He said he always carries two watches when he travels to another time zone. He sets one watch to the right time for the area he's visiting. The other is a Mickey Mouse watch his son gave him, set for the correct time back home."

"And the bicycle man?" Dr. Quicksolve said.

"He had a wallet and some change in his pockets. He also had a backpack attached to his bike with clothes in it. He said he was traveling across the state on a bicycle trip by himself. His bike had a headlight and a small tool kit that had just one wrench and a screwdriver. That's all he had. He said he was from out of town and that the other guy scared him when he pulled the knife out."

"The main suspect is obvious," Sergeant Shurshot said.

Dr. Quicksolve nodded his head in agreement.

Who is the best suspect?

Answer on page 92.

Stalling

etective Elliott Savant checked his suitcase in and got his tickets for his flight to Dallas from Detroit. Then he stood in line again at the entrance to the lobby that led to the gates at the security clearance. He had to present papers and identification showing that, in spite of his appearance with his young Albert Einstein look—wild, long, curly black hair—and his trench coat and galoshes, he really was a police officer, licensed to travel armed. He also presented papers for his short-legged companion, his pet bulldog, Marguerite. Again, the papers that declared Marguerite to be a police dog licensed to travel on the airline in a regular seat and not in a travel box, also seemed incongruous to her appearance. This incongruity was what made them a good pair. Still, it was hard to imagine a police dog that apparently could never manage to bite a perpetrator above the kneecaps, although she certainly did look intimidating—more like the stereotypical image of a cantankerous desk sergeant than an attack dog.

Suddenly a message came over the phones in the hands of the security guards telling them to clear the building. Immediately an announcement came over the loudspeakers to calmly clear the building. Flights would be delayed until a security matter was cleared up. People looked concerned, some looked frightened, but everyone reacted calmly and began leaving the building.

Elliott saw two sheriff deputies walking by quickly. He jogged through the metal detectors and caught up with them. Marguerite bounced along behind him, happy to have a little excitement.

Elliott showed them his identification and asked what was going on. One of the deputies pointed down the hall, where two security guards and another deputy were talking to a tall, dark-haired woman in a business suit. As they approached, they heard what she was saying.

"He kept shouting, 'I have a bomb! I have a bomb!' That was no bomb! He stole my cell phone! Then he ran in there." She pointed to a door marked "Men."

The two deputies drew their guns and dashed through the restroom door. Elliott paused to talk to the lady for minute. Then he casually strolled into the restroom behind the officers. Marguerite, with an air of importance, marched along behind him.

In the restroom, the deputies were standing side by side with their guns pointed at the three stalls.

"He must be in one of the stalls," one of the deputies said nervously.

"Can your dog tell us which one?" the other deputy said.

"She could," Elliott said. "But before we risk Marguerite's nose, let's try something else. The lady told me something that might help." He reached into his coat pocket.

What was Elliott reaching into his pocket for?

44

Mystery Party

The two-mile drive off the main road and through the foggy forest of tall pines set the stage for mystery—but when they entered the large hall, it looked almost like a Halloween party.

"It's more like who-dun-nuts!" Officer Boysenberry said to Junior as they looked across the large assembly in the Great Lodge that was in the center of the Custer State Park near Kalamazoo, Michigan. Moose and deer heads, trout, and huge salmon were hung on the walls. Entering guests were diverted to a room where several large tables had been pushed together to support the pile of coats.

The "nuts" Officer Boysenberry referred to were the forty or so people who stood around drinking hot tea, cider, and punch, and nibbling snacks. They were detective mystery fans, and many were dressed in costumes that represented their heroes. There were about twelve Sherlock Holmeses with the distinctive hunter's cap and heavy caped overcoat. A few other Sherlock Holmeses had taken off their hats and coats but still could easily be identified by their large-bowl pipes. Smoking was not allowed at the lodge, but that did not keep many of the Sherlocks from clenching a large pipe tightly between their teeth or waving it in the air to emphasize a point.

Other detectives, mostly fictional and from various eras, were represented. There were several television detectives who were pretty much indistinguishable from each other—Sergeant Fridays, Mannixes, Spencers, etc. Others had more individual characteristics—a bald-headed Kojak, Magnum, P. I.s, with their dark mustaches, and several Charlie Chans.

One famous detective, though, was not disguised at all. That is not to say he did not have a unique "costume." He was just himself. Detective Elliott Savant, with his rumpled trench coat, his shiny black galoshes, and his wild, curly hair and bushy black mustache, was as recognized and, indeed, as renowned as all the others because he was as eccentric and unique as any fictional detective. But he was real, and he was here.

Elliott was first discovered by the public as the partner of the famous, and famously discreet, Dr. J. L. Quicksolve. With his own unique ways of solving several crimes after Dr. Quicksolve left the police force, and, of course, his behavior and appearance, Detective Elliott Savant quickly became a legend in his

own right. Those peculiarities and his penchant for wandering off with his mind on six or seven things other than what he was doing at the moment prompted his bosses to assign an officer to tag along and keep an eye on him. Alvin Boysenberry was that very nervous officer.

Boysenberry had been quite anxious about attending this convention of mystery aficionados. Now that he was here, Boysenberry was surprised at how comfortable he actually felt. He attributed that to the amount of time he had spent with Detective Elliott Savant. He felt that probably prepared him for characters far more bizarre than these.

The first of several "mysteries" was not long in coming. Thunder roared out like an explosion. The door was slammed open. Lightning flashed and rain poured down behind a beautiful young woman in a large fur coat, who charged into the room. She paused to look heavenward and let out such a long, blood-curdling scream that it made Elliott wonder if she might be a swimmer or an opera singer to have such lungs. Then she began to cry out dramatically, "He's been shot! He's been shot! Freddie's been shot in the parking lot!"

"I bet that hurt," Elliott said to himself as the beautiful blonde slumped to the floor in a heap of raccoon fur.

The "Keystones" rushed in behind her. They were the "police" who were there to move things along while the guests were expected to really solve the crime. They were dressed like the Keystone Cops of the old silent movies.

"Did you see him?" one of the Keystones asked, searching the group with his eyes. "Someone saw the murderer run in here!" He took off his police cap and shook off the rainwater. "Who has a clue?" he shouted.

Nearly everyone in the room raised a hand and waited patiently for a turn to comment.

"Yes," the policeman said, pointing to a Sherlock Holmes who held his pipe in the air.

"The coats!" he said with a British accent that made you wonder what part of Canada he might be from. "The pile of coats!" he said. "The last person to come in would have thrown his coat on top of the pile." Several people smiled and nodded their heads, obviously agreeing with this clever deduction.

"Maybe not," someone said. Everyone turned to look at Detective Elliott Savant. "There is a better way, if that idea fails," Elliott said.

What could Elliott mean?

Answer on pages 92–93.

Boysenberry's Burglary

Detective Elliott Savant had a passion for exotic vehicles. He usually had a very unusual antique car or a custom hot rod that he drove when he was not riding his motorcycle. He also liked parades. As a matter of fact, he combined his pleasures every year when he drove his car in the Fourth of July Parade. He usually let his friend Junior Quicksolve and Junior's twin cousins, Flora and Fauna, ride along with him in the parade. They enjoyed throwing candy out to the children in the crowd that lined the streets along the parade route.

Junior and his cousins sat on the porch of Junior's house, anxiously waiting for "Uncle" Elliott to pick them up.

"I can't wait to see Elliott's car," Junior said.

"He gets a new one almost every year, doesn't he?" Flora said.

"A different one, you mean," Fauna corrected her sister.

"Yes," Flora said. "They are almost always old and strange."

"But they look like new," Fauna said.

Junior had just opened his mouth to list all the antique cars he could remember Elliott had driven in the annual parade. But before he could start to talk, they heard a loud, high-pitched screech of squealing tires, and they looked up to see a low-slung black car race around the corner and come blasting toward them. The car looked like it was on fire as it roared up to them. Smoke billowed from its spinning tires and bright red flames were painted across its hood and fenders. When the car slammed to a stop right in front of them, it seemed to sink down and settle to within a few inches of the pavement.

"A '49 Mercury!" Junior said.

"That's right!" Elliott said through the open windows. "Hop in!"

The kids piled in, and the car screeched away from the house, spinning the tires and leaving a long tail of smoke behind them.

"Your tires are not going to last long," Junior said with a big grin.

"You're right," Elliott said, "and I don't want to get a ticket." He slowed down to well below the speed limit as if that would be his apology for his naughty behavior. "A policeman should not get a ticket," he said.

Reacting to the sudden slowdown, Flora looked

back and forth at each side of the street and quipped,
"Are we in the parade already?"

"I don't see the people!" Fauna said, jumping in on
the joke.

"Maybe if we throw candy!" Junior said. He reached
into the bag of candy that sat on the floor between his
feet and threw a handful of candy out the window
toward the curb. Everyone laughed.

It was not long, though, before they actually were in
the parade, waving to the crowd of people who lined
the streets and throwing candy to real children who
scampered around to get their share.

Suddenly Junior noticed someone huffing and
puffing as he jogged along beside their car. He wore a
dark blue policeman's uniform. It was Officer
Boysenberry.

"Detective Savant! Detective Savant!" Boysenberry
said.

"What is it?" Elliott said to the officer who continued to trot along beside their car. "And why are you running along like this?"

"That's just it," Boysenberry said, huffing and puffing as he tried to keep up. "My car has been stolen!"

"Stolen?" Elliott said.

"Stolen," Boysenberry said.

"Where was it stolen?" Elliott said.

"From my garage," Boysenberry said, clinging to the side of the car with one hand.

Junior could not help but smile at the comical contrast of Elliott's cool and calm demeanor as he drove along in the middle of a parade and Boysenberry's distress as he jogged along gasping for breath in near panic about losing his car.

"That is not all," Boysenberry said. "They took my wallet."

"Your wallet?" Elliott said.

Boysenberry hesitated, trying to catch his breath. "My wallet," he said.

"Where did they get your wallet?" Elliott asked.

"Out of my pants," Boysenberry gasped, apparently growing tired from the running.

"Your pants?" Elliott asked. He waved to someone he recognized in the crowd on the sidewalk.

Boysenberry waved too, without looking. "My pants," he said.

"They got into…my house," Boysenberry panted. He could barely finish his sentences now. "They took my wallet, and they took my car while I was asleep."

"How did they get in?" Elliott said.

"I don't know," Boysenberry said.

"Did they break in?" Elliott said.

"No," Boysenberry said.

"Where had you been?" Elliott said, "Before you went to bed, I mean."

"We went to a restaurant to celebrate my birthday," Boysenberry said.

"Ah!" Elliott said.

Junior had been listening closely and chimed in, "Ah!"

Boysenberry's eyebrows went up when he looked at Junior in the back seat, but he did not have the energy to ask what Junior's "Ah!" was about.

"Did someone park your car at the restaurant?" Junior asked. "Did you give someone your keys?"

"Ah!" Boysenberry said.

Junior smiled.

Then Boysenberry said, "No, not my house keys, if that is what you think. The valet did not copy my house key and sneak in that way. I took the car key off my key ring. He did not get the house key."

"But how else?" Junior said.

"Through the garage," Elliott said.

"But how could he get into the garage?" Boysenberry said.

How could the parking valet have gotten into Boysenberry's garage to get into the house?

Answer on page 93.

Axe-Throwing Pioneers

Dr. J. L. Quicksolve and Detective Elliott Savant looked like brothers of the frontier. The two tall, lanky figures stood in their buckskin outfits in an opening in a forest of trees. Elliott, who looked like the younger brother because of his dark hair and bushy mustache, was nearly covered in leather from head to toe except for the Davy Crockett-style coonskin cap made of raccoon fur with the striped tail hanging down the back. Dr. Quicksolve was also in buckskin, with fringe along the arms of his jacket that fluttered and made a whooshing sound as his arm came down and he released the large axe that went twirling like an airplane propeller. It landed...

Whack!…in the middle of a target marked on a tree several yards away.

"A tie!" Junior shouted.

Junior and his twin cousins, Flora and Fauna, stood back behind a rope line that held the spectators back a safe distance from the axe-throwing competition.

They were all at the Kris Crossing Frontier Days Celebration in a large camping area ten miles out from the small town where Dr. Quicksolve grew up.

"One throw each to decide the winner," the judge said.

Elliott went first, swinging his axe back with his left arm. He stepped forward with a long, graceful stride and brought his arm down with a forceful snap. The axe spun away with a Whoosh!… and again, as his last throw had, whacked into the center of the target.

Dr. Quicksolve stepped up to the stake that marked where he was to stand. He reached back and let his axe fly just as the woods filled with the screech of sirens.

Everyone looked up as several police cars and an ambulance streamed into camp. As the vehicles stopped and the officers were piling out, everyone looked back to see what had happened to Dr. Quicksolve's throw. Amazingly, his axe had split the handle of Elliott's axe, landing, in effect, exactly on center in the same spot.

"So you are Robin Hood now," Elliott joked and laughed.

There was no joking about the reason for the sudden arrival of police cars. A man had been stabbed at a tent site just a quarter mile away. Suspects had been apprehended.

Sergeant Shurshot explained that two men were

there to camp and fish for the weekend. As they were brought out of the police cars, it could be seen that they each had leather sheaths attached to their belts.

"We took their hunting knives," Sergeant Shurshot said. "We will take them to the lab to be tested."

"So there was no weapon left at the scene?" Elliott asked.

"No," Sergeant Shurshot said. "The wound indicates he was probably stabbed with a knife."

The other suspect was being brought up to the group of officers and detectives at that moment. His wife was following them, protesting loudly. "My husband does not have a hunting knife!" she shouted.

"He did not have a knife on him," the officer said, holding the man's arm.

"We are just out here fishing for a few days. We always come out to the festival to eat some fish and watch stuff," the woman said.

Sergeant Shurshot turned to Dr. Quicksolve and Elliott and, speaking quietly, said, "Well, it looks like the best suspects are the guys with the knives. The tests will tell us which one is the murder weapon."

"Or not," Elliott said.

"Not is most likely," Dr. Quicksolve said.

"What?" Sergeant Shurshot said.

What, indeed, are Dr. Quicksolve and Elliott saying?

Answer on page 93.

Boogerman

"**Some days are too nice for crime**," Officer Boysenberry said as he turned on the police siren and quickly checked traffic, made a U-turn with his black-and-white police car, and sped down the road. They had just received a call about an accident and a possible shooting.

"A nice day can definitely be spoiled," Detective Elliott Savant said. He sat on the passenger side of the police car and concentrated on keeping his cup of coffee balanced so the hot liquid would not spill onto his lap. His Howdy Doody cup seemed to dance in the air. Coffee splashed up with each bump in the pavement.

They arrived at the scene where a blue sedan was pulled far to the right and off the road. The left front fender was severely crumpled, but the other vehicle involved in the crash was not there. There were two police cars and an ambulance. Lights flashed from the emergency vehicles and radios rumbled and squawked, creating a noisy, eerie picture.

Officer Longarm was on the scene. He opened the car door for Elliott when he saw the detective had his hands full with his hot coffee. Officer Longarm began giving Elliott the details of the situation even before he was out of the car.

"A man has been shot. He is dead. It could be road rage or a planned murder," Officer Longarm said. "The other driver apparently crossed the road to hit this one. It looks like the accident was his fault."

"No apparent reason for him to be angry," Elliott, said. "Have you found the car? A suspect? The weapon?" Elliott asked, his mind apparently going off in several directions at once.

"The gun was in the victim's car," Officer Longarm said as he and Boysenberry trotted along beside Elliott who marched around the car, peered into the window at the victim, and finally climbed up on the hood. He walked along the fender and stepped over the wind-shield to stand on the roof of the car to look around and survey the scene.

Officer Longarm had stopped talking and stood there looking up at Elliott.

"Go ahead," Elliott said.

Officer Longarm composed himself and continued. "They found the other car right around the corner there." He pointed his ink pen in the direction of the nearest corner. A comic book store prevented them from seeing the other car. Two emergency medics

rounded the corner toward them and walked over to stand between the two police officers. All four of them were staring up at Elliott, who took a presidential pose as if he were George Washington crossing the Delaware River. He looked down at the two medics, whose mouselike faces were familiar to him. They looked like they could have been twins. The female medic began talking immediately when she saw she had Elliott's attention.

"We got here right away," she said in a squeaky voice. "We were very close. We didn't see the accident..."

"But we heard the shot," the man said.

"Did you see any suspects?" Boysenberry asked.

"No," Miss Medic said. "We saw two men walking away," Miss Medic explained, "but that doesn't make them suspects."

"Boogerman!" Mr. Medic said. "He looked suspicious!"

"Pardon me," Boysenberry said.

"Boogerman," Mr. Medic said. "He was picking his..."

"No, he wasn't!" Miss Medic said.

"He was flicking!" Mr. Medic said.

"Flicking isn't picking!" she said.

"You have to pick to flick!" he insisted.

"Excuse me," Boysenberry said.

The two little people settled down.

Mr. Medic said, "The Boogerman went that way." He pointed down the street.

"The other guy went that way," Miss Medic said, as if her guy were the better suspect.

"And what was suspicious about this other guy?" Officer Longarm asked.

"He was tall," Miss Medic said.

"That doesn't make him suspicious!" Mr. Medic insisted.

"He was tall," she repeated. "All I am saying…he was tall."

The two officers looked up at Detective Savant for help.

"Were either of them wearing gloves?" Elliott asked.

"No," the medics said.

"Look for the Boogerman first," Elliott said to the officers.

Why the Boogerman?

Answers on page 93–94.

Puffblossom Gets the Blame

Detective Elliott Savant was quite a sight in his red-and-white cowboy outfit. He was still decked out with his riding chaps that were leather covered in sheepskin on the front. The cottony white wool made it look like Elliott's long, thin legs were skewered into giant marshmallows. He liked to tell people he didn't wear them just to look funny. They were authentic. Real cowboys wore them to protect their legs from brush and to keep them warm. He also wore bright red cowboy boots with silver eagles on the sides and a matching red leather vest, white shirt, and a nearly white cowboy hat to show he was a good guy. He and his dancing mule, Mollie, had been in the

Fourth of July parade. Elliott was backing the animal out of his horse trailer when Officer Alvin Boysenberry raced up to him.

"Someone has been killed!" Boysenberry shouted. Then he filled in the details. Butch Springrock, the famous country western rap singer, had been found dead in the stall of the notorious stallion, Puffblossom. He looked like he had been stomped to death.

"Are there any human suspects?" Elliott asked, twirling his silver six-guns as if that would help him concentrate.

"Most country western rappers have a lot of people who disagree with their music style. Butch Springrock was no exception. But the most likely suspect would be his manager, Hank Yerchain. He has been pretty upset with Butch for refusing to do concerts in Tibet. Butch was afraid of flying in an airplane and was talking about getting a new agent. Well, look at this!"

Boysenberry recognized the yellow Corvette pulling into the long driveway to the stables. They watched as a tall, skinny man with a tiny head, tiny dots for eyes, and a very thin mustache that looked like it was penciled in just above his upper lip climbed out of the sports car. It was Butch Springrock's agent, Hank Yerchain.

"What's up?" the man said.

"Bad news," Officer Boysenberry said. "Butch Springrock has had an accident. He's dead."

Suddenly, "Blam! Blam! Blam!" The shots continued as Boysenberry and Hank Yerchain turned to see Elliott firing his two revolvers repeatedly, one after the other. Across the yard a metal bucket danced in the air, kept suspended by the continuous firing.

The shooting stopped, and the bucket came down with a final thud.

Boysenberry, accustomed to surprises from Elliott, continued talking as if the noisy interruption was not an unusual thing at all. "Butch was…"

"Oh, no! I told him to be careful!" Hank shouted. "I told him to stay away from Puffblossom! That Puffblossom is a killer horse!"

"You are his agent?" Elliott asked, twirling his ivory-handled revolvers into their holsters.

"Who are you?" Hank asked Elliott.

"Detective Elliott Savant," Boysenberry said, as if Elliott could not answer for himself while he was wearing his cowboy outfit.

"It might not be an accident," Elliott said, quietly patting Mollie's gray flank.

"What does that mean?" the agent demanded. "Do you think he was murdered? Who would do that?"

"I think you might," Elliott said bluntly.

"I was upset about his fear of flying," Hank Yerchain said. "But I need him. He's my biggest client!"

"So there must be quite an insurance policy," Boysenberry said.

"But he's worth more to me alive and performing," the agent argued. "You have no reason to suspect me!"

"Actually," Elliott said, "we have a good reason besides the motive. I don't think it was Puffblossom's dislike of country rap that led to this murder."

Why suspect the agent?

Answer on page 94.

Custom Masseys

Detective Elliott Savant and Officer Boysenberry were in the large, six-car garage of professional golfer Neal Putterstar. Neal was very tall and blonde and handsome, except for the fact he had once ripped off his left ear and thrown it into a pond when he missed a putt. He later claimed it made him a better golfer because the way the wind whistled through the little stub that was left helped him decide how to play his longer shots.

Officer Boysenberry noticed Putterstar's straw hat rested on his ear on the left side, but it slipped down on the right where there was no ear to stop its descent. It nearly covered his right eye, and Boysenberry wondered why it did not interfere with his golfing.

They were questioning Neal about the theft of his treasured, custom-made golf clubs. At least Boysenberry was asking questions. Elliott had borrowed a spare putter to practice at the other end of the garage where there was a putting green set up with artificial grass and three holes to putt into. Officer Boysenberry looked across the garage at Elliott, who seemed to be paying no attention to the job at hand. Boysenberry wondered why Elliott had rolled his pant legs up to his knees to practice putting. It did not upset him, though, as many other things that Elliott did often could. Boysenberry was just happy Elliott had decided not to wear his galoshes on this hot summer day. The jingle of the buckles always disturbed Boysenberry's concentration.

Elliott was currently stretched out under a large, deep blue Mercedes, trying to reach a wayward golf ball with his putter.

"Every time I come home from playing, I like to clean my golf clubs and set them out on this rack," Neal Putterstar said.

Boysenberry looked up from his notebook to see that the beautiful oak rack, which was obviously made just to display this set of golf clubs, was now empty.

"They were my favorite clubs," Neal said. "My best clubs," he continued. "They were B. and J. Masseys... custom made." Neal appeared to be on the brink of tears, speaking of his golf clubs in the past tense.

Although it looked like Elliott had not been listening, apparently he had been and was touched by Neal's emotional display. He walked back over to Neal and said, "Do you suspect anyone in particular?"

"Yes," Neal said. "Sadly, I am sure it was one of my nephews. They are visiting from Ferndale. They are right outside. And their cars are outside. I am pretty sure my clubs are in the trunk of one of those cars. I am just reluctant to accuse either of them. They both have been talking about how they would like to be professional golfers. They seemed to think that if they only had a set of B. and J. Masseys like mine, they could be golf stars. They are both decent golfers, but good clubs won't make them professionals."

Officer Boysenberry and Elliott looked at each other with puzzled expressions. "Your nephews?" Elliott said to Neal.

"Out here," Neal said, pointing toward a door that led to the backyard.

They went into the backyard where they saw two young men playing catch with a baseball. One was very short and bald. He was winding up and throwing the ball like a pitcher. "Strike!" the other one shouted as the ball struck his catcher's mitt with a loud cracking sound. Any baseball fan would have noticed the unusual catcher's mitt—not just because it was very large, like the ones catchers use with a knuckleball pitcher, but because it was left-handed. Apparently, there was a lot of custom sports equipment around here.

"Well," Officer Boysenberry said. It is easy to tell which nephew is most likely to have taken your clubs to use himself."

"Which one?" Neal said.

"Probably neither," Elliott said.

Why did Boysenberry think he knew who took the clubs? Why did Elliott say, "Probably neither"?

Answer on page 94.

Snubnose Smith

Officer Boysenberry wheeled the black-and-white police car around the corner that brought them immediately out of the city and into what appeared to be another world altogether. It was a wealthy neighborhood of long, green lawns that led up to circular drives in front of huge stone and brick mansions. Detective Elliott Savant called them "starter castles." Boysenberry said they looked pretty much like full-fledged castles to him.

Elliott explained why they were in this wealthy neighborhood as they drove up a long, winding drive

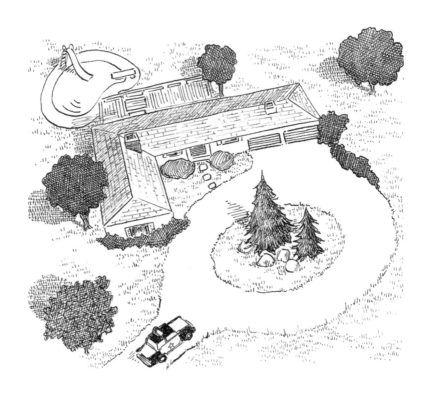

toward one of the larger homes. "Bob 'Snubnose' Smith has been blackmailing his mob bosses," Elliott said. "He has been threatening them with a list of names he said includes mob associates and activities. The list tells who did what crimes in the mob over the past two years. We want to get that list before they get to him."

Just as they reached the house, they heard a loud explosion and saw a huge flash of light. The garage door sailed over the police car and clattered down on the driveway behind them. It skidded down the drive another thirty yards before it flipped over onto the lawn.

The smoke cleared quickly. There was no fire. They saw what looked like a blackened figure in the shape of a man. It looked to be made of ashes, still smoldering from the explosion. The figure was standing like a statue over an equally blackened lawn mower, a strange piece of artwork depicting suburban life.

"Is that a man?" Boysenberry asked.

Suddenly they heard a siren, and a small turquoise-and-white Rambler automobile with a flashing red light pulled up beside them. Two short, dark-haired people in medics' uniforms jumped out of the car. Elliott and Boysenberry recognized them from previous cases. The two medics, a man and a woman, looked like brother and sister with their small, mouse-like faces.

"How did you get here so fast?" Boysenberry asked.

"We were in the neighborhood," the woman said.

"You are…" Elliott began.

"Medics," the man said.

"I know," Elliott said, "but…"

"People get us confused," the woman said.

"I am sure that is easy to do," Elliott said.

"Mixed up," the little man said. "She means people get us mixed up."

"I am sure that is easy to do," Elliott repeated.

"They have trouble with the names," the woman said.

"Names?" Elliott said.

"Names," the man said. "Our names…they're alike…Mattie and Matthew."

"I am Mattie," the woman said.

"I am Matthew," the man said.

"What about this?" Elliott said, pointing to the smoldering figure.

Matthew peered into what looked like the face of the figure. "Dead," he said. "He's dead."

They heard a loud noise and turned to see a large garbage truck coming up the street.

"They're coming to get him already," Matthew said.

"That's not an ambulance," Mattie said. "That's a garbage truck!"

Suddenly the door to the house opened, and a young, attractive blonde in white shorts and a white blouse with red hearts came out. She stopped in surprise and looked around at everyone standing in her garage. She had earphones on her head that covered her ears. She pulled them off her head and let them drop to her neck. She reached to her side to a switch and turned down the volume. She stared at the burned figure. She said, "They finally got him. I thought I heard something." Then she turned and grabbed a large plastic garbage can and began dragging it to the end of the circular drive. "Garbage day," she said.

"We were wondering if you know anything about a list!" Boysenberry shouted to her.

She left the garbage can at the curb and came back to get another one. She paused to answer the question. "No." Then she dragged the second garbage can to the curb. When she returned, she said, "I don't know about that list. I don't think he would have threatened those guys if he didn't have a list. On the other hand, a list like that is something he wouldn't want left lying around if something happened to him. It would have things on it he would not want people to find out about...who committed crimes and stuff...like his

mother maybe…he wouldn't want people to know about his mother."

Mattie and Matthew looked at each other with wide-eyed expressions and then stared at Mrs. Smith.

"So," Elliott said. "You think there's a list, but he would have wanted it destroyed if something happened to him?"

"That's it," Mrs. Smith said.

"Maybe it's in his pocket," Boysenberry said. They all looked at the figure that was beginning to disintegrate into a pile of ashes on the concrete floor.

"No pockets," Mattie said.

"He probably knew he could have been kidnapped and searched," Elliott said. "He wouldn't have carried it with him. He would want it hidden where he could get it easily after they paid him off, but where it would disappear if something happened to him.

"Then I guess we aren't going to find it," Boysenberry said.

"That might depend on how fast we move right now," Elliott said.

What did Elliott mean?

Answer on page 94.

𝔇ragon

After examining the body, Officer Beekerjar solemnly said, "Foul play," as if someone might have thought the victim lying along the path that snaked through a clump of trees in City Center Park might have been shot three times in the heart by accident.

With his long, curly black hair blowing frantically in the wind, Detective Elliott Savant brushed his black mustache with his fingers as he began walking in circles, looking down at the ground. You could not tell if he was looking for clues or simply deep in thought.

Officer Boysenberry stood nervously watching Elliott. "Well," Boysenberry said, scratching his head as if he might dig up an idea.

"Somebody sure can shoot," Officer Lurkin said, apparently feeling some kind of conclusion had to be drawn.

"What have we found so far?" Boysenberry asked Officer Lurkin.

"We've identified the suspect. He is Donnie Dymolsky. He is called Donnie Dime on the street. He's been working with the police as an informer. Apparently, some bad guys didn't like what he had to say about them. The local hoodlums, as you know, have used a certain enforcer, a hitman named Dragon. It looks like it could be Dragon who killed Donnie Dime. He's been the suspect in killings like this before. He's never been charged. There are always clues, but there are so many conflicting clues that it's hard to figure out what happened and put it all together. He might have slipped up this time, though. We found three nine-millimeter casings right here to the left of the path. He used an automatic and didn't pick up the shells."

"If we find his gun, we might match it to markings on the shells," Beekerjar said.

Officer Lurkin continued, "It looks like Donnie Dime was walking down this path. Somebody came up behind him. He turned around." Officer Lurkin pointed down the sloping hill toward the body. He pointed his finger as if to dramatize the incident. "Then he was shot."

"The shells?" Elliott said.

"They were here to our left," Officer Lurkin said. He pointed to the ground at a narrow spot between the path and a tall tree.

Elliott bent down and picked up a sandwich bag that

lay on the ground near the tree. He held it up to the sunlight, examining it closely.

"What are you looking for?" Officer Lurkin said.

"Crumbs," Elliott said.

"Hungry?" Boysenberry asked.

"No," Elliott replied. "I don't expect to find crumbs."

What was Elliott thinking?

Answer on pages 94–95.

Bigbert and Spud

Everyone at Southside Elementary School was having a good time at their annual American Heritage Carnival. Both kids and adults walked around the playground and inside the school wearing a huge variety of costumes that represented the people of America throughout history. There were British soldiers, colonial statesmen, pilots, rock stars, hippies—everything America's rich culture has had to offer through its people of various origins and backgrounds. There were games and booths and rides and shows.

One of the most popular shows was an Old West roping demonstration being put on by our very own Detective Elliott Savant and his now-famous dancing mule, Mollie.

Mollie wore her finest shiny black-leather saddle with sparkling silver conches. Elliott wore his parade outfit, complete with a tall, white ten-gallon cowboy hat and his trademark puffy, white lambskin chaps. His tall, red boots were etched with a beautiful design with large, silver eagles.

Elliott was standing on Mollie's back doing rope tricks, twirling his lariat in a large circle above his head. He kept letting out more rope, making the circle larger and larger. Finally he stopped and brought the spinning circle of rope slowly down over both himself and his mule, Mollie, who stood rock steady. The spinning circle of rope touched the ground and quickly shot up into the air above them again.

At that moment, Elliott felt a tingling in his vest pocket that meant his cell phone was vibrating. He reached into his pocket with one hand while the other hand kept the rope spinning above his head. Elliott pulled a small device from his pocket. He stuck one end of the device, an earphone, into his ear, and the other end of it wrapped around his cheek so he could speak into the tiny microphone and keep his hands free.

Things were not so happy on the business side of town. Officer Boysenberry stood in a downtown parking garage. He was talking on a cell phone to

Elliott, explaining the situation. A body lay nearby, covered with a blanket. Medics and officers moved around the crime scene. Two men were in separate police cars, being questioned.

"Bigbert of Bigbert and Spud Potatoes has been murdered. He was stabbed," Boysenberry told Elliott.

Elliott brought his spinning lariat down to a more manageable size as he listened to Boysenberry's report. He brought it to a perpendicular angle to his left and began bringing it back and forth, left to right and back, jumping through the circle and landing back on the saddle he was standing on, deftly maintaining his balance as he listened to the grim description of the crime scene. The crowd roared and applauded.

Boysenberry explained that Bigbert was clubbed

and stabbed by two men as he got into his car. A witness who was on the other end of the parking structure saw the two men, but he did not get a good look at their faces. He yelled for them to stop and ran toward them, but they ran away.

The surprising thing, Boysenberry said, was the man also saw Bigbert's partner, Spencer Spud, standing by his own car, watching his partner being mugged. The witness claimed Spud watched for at least a minute and then jumped into his car and drove away. Someone else must have called the police. They arrived just as Mr. Spud was pulling out of the parking structure. They stopped him for questioning. His story was that he saw the mugging and was so frightened he had trouble with the keys to his car when he tried getting into it. It was a large, expensive Cadillac, and he was afraid he would be mugged and carjacked. He said he was going to get help when the police arrived.

"Arrest him," Elliott said as he jumped through the circle the last time. He threw his hands up into the air, and the crowd applauded.

Why did Elliott say to arrest Spencer Spud?

Answer on page 95.

Uncle's Will

Dr. J. L. Quicksolve and Sergeant Rebekah Shurshot sat in the Coffee Clatch Café in downtown Ann Arbor. They sat in a small booth near the window. Sergeant Shurshot was drinking coffee and eating a chocolate-covered donut. Dr. Quicksolve was drinking tea and eyeing Sergeant Shurshot's donut.

"So you gave up donuts?" Sergeant Shurshot said.

"I am cutting back," Dr. Quicksolve said.

He looked across Main Street at a large construction site. Actually, it was a huge hole.

"A hole that large means an awfully big building," he said, as much to change the subject as anything else.

"Ten stories," Sergeant Shurshot said.

"Some people think congestion is a good thing," Dr. Quicksolve said.

"Yes," Sergeant Shurshot said, "people who make cold medicine."

Dr. Quicksolve smiled for a second at this rare piece of humor, one with two meanings even, from Sergeant Shurshot. His smile disappeared, and he said soberly, "I wonder how many fire engines we have with ladders that will reach ten stories."

"Or how many people would die trying to walk down ten flights of stairs in a burning building," Sergeant Shurshot said.

"Well," Dr. Quicksolve said, trying to change the subject again. "I don't think you invited me here to talk about donuts or congestion or sweet nothings."

"Sweet nothings would be my first choice," Sergeant Shurshot said. "But you are right. It is business. We got a call from Baltimore. Tom Wyatt from the Baltimore Police Department said the billionaire

media mogul, Travis Eastpointe, is terrified."

"That wealthy recluse is always terrified, isn't he?" Dr. Quicksolve said.

"Specifically," Sergeant Shurshot said, "he is afraid of his nephew, Jason Moline, who lives right here in town. He said Jason called him a few days ago and threatened his life when he found out his uncle was going to change his will this Friday and leave Jason with nothing. Jason has been pulled in for several violence- and gun-related charges before, but his lawyers have always gotten him off the hook. He looks to be a real threat."

"Why don't we go have a talk with Mr. Moline?" Dr. Quicksolve said.

"I knew you would say that," Sergeant Shurshot said.

"People are going to begin to talk about how well you know me," Dr. Quicksolve said.

Sergeant Shurshot laughed and said, "Captain Rootumout is getting a search warrant. He will meet us at Jason Moline's house in an hour. Enjoy your tea."

Jason Moline lived on a secluded gravel road north of town. The houses were mostly separated by some distance, but Jason did have a neighbor directly across the street. Their mailboxes were each set at the end of their driveways. They seemed to face each other like two soldiers on sentry duty. The blue plastic newspaper cylinders added color to their uniforms.

Sergeant Shurshot turned the police car into the short driveway, where they found Captain Rootumout and Officer Longarm standing in the yard talking to Mr. Jason Moline. In front of the police car was a blue

sedan with the trunk gaping open. Officer Longarm
walked to their car and began talking as soon as Dr.
Quicksolve opened the door to step out.

"We found a revolver, a scoped rifle, and ammu-
nition in the trunk of Jason's car," Officer Longarm
said.

They heard the rumble of a vehicle on the gravel
road and turned to see a red pickup truck drive by,

spewing sand and gravel into the air behind it.

Officer Longarm paused for the truck to pass because the noise interfered with their discussion. "Jason said he was planning on going to the shooting range. The handgun is registered, and he has a permit." Officer Longarm paused again as the same red truck drove by the other way, stopping for a second this time to put a newspaper in the neighbor's blue tube.

"Why don't we go inside to talk?" Sergeant Shurshot suggested as another vehicle passed by quickly. This time it was a small mail truck.

"What did he say about his uncle?" Dr. Quicksolve asked, obviously hesitant to walk toward the house with the others.

"He said he loves his uncle and hopes he lives forever," Officer Longarm said.

The mail truck came back the other way, stopping at the neighbor's mailbox.

"Yes. Let's go inside," Dr. Quicksolve said.

After they were inside and introductions were finished, Dr. Quicksolve asked Jason a question: "Were you coming from or going to target practice?"

"I am going shooting later today," Jason said. "Why do you ask me that? Don't you believe I am going to go shooting?"

"Yes. I think you plan to go shooting," Dr. Quicksolve said, "in Baltimore. Though I suppose you will get off the hook this time too. At least your uncle will get his will changed on Friday."

What was Dr. Quicksolve talking about?

Answer on page 95.

Answers

Vanished Vase (page 6)—Hilary could only know the beautiful vase was only worth twenty dollars if she had stolen it and tried to sell it. She knew, as she had said, "it was not worth stealing," because she had stolen it and found out!

Chewing Gum Art (page 9)—Dr. Quicksolve, like everyone else, heard three separate Chrrrk! sounds of the drills. But there were six screws. That means there must have been two men working together and turning on their drills at the same time to remove the six screws. It looked like both men were involved, not just one!

Cousin in Custody (page 13)—All that cleaning may have been done to cover up evidence. Painting the basement floor without being asked looks especially suspicious. He may have been trying to cover bloodstains on the concrete floor.

Crime Time (page 16)—Junior knew Skeeter was right, and John Bigdood was pretty smart, but if he did not know that Skeeter had had the watch a long time, he might not think to open the watch and wipe off what should be a nice set of Skeeter's fingerprints on the battery.

Robbins (page 20)—Dr. Quicksolve was referring to the telephone repairman who had a name so similar to the inventor of the telephone. He believed that a man who worked with tools and probably had a set of tools strapped around his waist could have removed the hinges or the door lock, if there was one, from inside the closet and escaped in that two-and-a-half-hour time period. Of course, being locked up like that gave him the appearance of innocence that he wanted!

Deputy Dowd (page 24)—Dowd claimed he started training to be a deputy for the Michigan State Police. In Michigan, as in other states, the state police officers are called officers or troopers. It is the county police who are called deputy sheriffs.

Go with the Flow (page 27)—Sergeant Shurshot figured the men in the second tent were lying about setting up the tent that morning before the rain because of the wet grass under their feet. Elliott realized what she was thinking and decided to check the tent to see if it was sitting on a slope or a depressed spot where water could flow into the tent during a heavy rain. He knew the wet grass did not necessarily mean it was not dry when the tent was set up!

When Turning Left Is Right (page 30)—Dr. Quicksolve had just left a one-way northbound street. He turned left, went one block, and turned right. The man instructed him to turn right twice. That would put them on a one-way street going the wrong way! Those instructions made it look like this was, indeed, a stranger from out of town who was just trying to get rid of them!

Friday Fudgesicle (page 33)—Dr. Quicksolve knew

the car was like his VW. Sidney had not put gas in it yet. He always got gas on Friday. Living forty miles away and filling the tank once a week meant there was quite a good chance that car did not even have enough gas to get to the next freeway exit!

Stalker (page 36)—If John Bigdood was stalking someone from his car at night, he might have thought to remove the dome lightbulb so the light didn't come on and give him away when he was getting in and out of his car. Lucy's story sounded like the car remained dark when the stalker got in, supporting Junior's theory.

Convenience Store Panic (page 39)—The running man might be a little goofy with the two watches, but there is no particular reason to suspect him. The bicycle man is a better suspect. He seems to be trying to look like a man on a bicycle trip, but he is missing a very important item—a tire pump! Chances are, he had a car waiting nearby.

Stalling (page 42)—Elliott was reaching for his cell phone. He got the woman's number and planned to dial it. The woman's phone would ring, telling them which stall the man was hiding in so they could deal with him as quickly and safely as possible.

Mystery Party (page 45)—Elliott knew that several mysteries from different authors have used this idea— the last one to enter would be the one to throw his coat on the top of the pile. But, knowing that, our culprit may well have stuffed his coat under the others to avoid detection. He could not change the fact that it must have just begun to rain. So his coat would also be wet. If the top coat was not wet, it would be wise to search for a coat with wet shoulders, showing that the owner had just come in from the rain.

Boysenberry's Burglary (page 50)—If Officer Alvin Boysenberry had an electric garage door opener in his car like many people have, the valet could have made a note of the settings so he could later go to Boysenberry's house and use a similar door opener to get into the garage. Once inside, he could easily have entered the house through the unlocked door, since most people don't lock their house door to what they think is a safely locked garage. The burglar wouldn't have needed a key to get in, and he could have gotten a key to the car once he was inside the house!

Axe-Throwing Pioneers (page 55)—They believed it was unlikely that the killer would hang onto the murder weapon long enough to get caught with it. He or she would have tossed it away or hidden it. The fact that the two men still had their knives led to doubts that either of these knives was the murder weapon— or that either man was the murderer. The other man said he was there to camp and fish. He must at least have brought a cooking knife. If he had no knife, he became the number one suspect. He couldn't clean, prepare, and eat fish very well without a knife!

Boogerman (page 59)—Since the gun was left at the scene and no one was wearing gloves, it looked like a planned murder by someone who was not worried about fingerprints on the gun. Since Boogerman was "flicking" something away with his fingers, Elliott suspected he had something on his fingertips, glue for example, that would prevent his leaving fingerprints on the weapon or the car. If he was caught before he washed his hands, there might have been a residue that would serve as evidence!

Puffblossom Gets the Blame (page 64)—Hank Yerchain immediately spoke about the "killer horse," Puffblossom, when he was told Butch was dead. Hank was not told Butch was found in Puffblossom's stall. It looks like the agent might have had Butch beaten to death and his body left in the stall to make it look like the horse had killed him!

Custom Masseys (page 67)—Boysenberry noticed one nephew was left-handed and would not be able to use the clubs of most golfers. Elliott noticed that too, and he also saw the other nephew was short. He would not be able to use clubs that were made for such a tall man!

Snubnose Smith (page 71)—Elliott figured out the perfect place to hide something so it would disappear if something happened to Snubnose—in the garbage cans! They needed to get them back before the garbage was hauled away!

Dragon (page 77)—Elliott did not believe an experienced hitman like Dragon would leave such obvious clues as spent shells that could be traced to his gun. Knowing Dragon's reputation for leaving false clues—

and the fact that an automatic pistol would throw the shells to the right and not the left—Elliott thought Dragon brought these shell casings, which came from a different gun in the bag he found, and left them as false clues!

Bigbert and Spud (page 80)—Mr. Spud had a brand-new, expensive car. It most likely would have a remote button that could be used quickly instead of a key. It also would have a "panic button" that would sound an alarm that might scare away the muggers. Finally, it quite likely would have an onboard system that could be used to get help immediately. Mr. Spud's story was hard to believe. Probably he was involved in the mugging of his business partner.

Uncle's Will (page 84)—Dr. Quicksolve noticed that the paper delivery man and the mail truck did not stop at Jason Moline's house. Apparently, he had stopped deliveries for some time. Added to the reported threat and the guns in the trunk, it looked like Jason might have been planning to drive to Baltimore and kill his uncle! Now the police will keep an eye on him until his uncle has time to change his will!

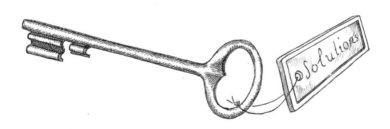

Index

Answer pages are in italics.